CORAL REEF

A City That Never Sleeps

CORAL REEF

A City That Never Sleeps

Text by
Mary M. Cerullo

Photographs by
Jeffrey L. Rotman

COBBLEHILL BOOKS
Dutton   New York

*To Arthur, my favorite diurnal and
nocturnal companion—MMC*

For Asher Gal, my dive buddy—JLR

ACKNOWLEDGMENTS

Many thanks to Dr. Joseph Levine, biologist and author of *The Coral Reef at Night*, and to Dr. Larry Harris, professor of zoology at the University of New Hampshire, for their review of the manuscript and helpful suggestions. Any mistakes are the author's alone.

Diagram of coral polyp on page 8 by Dr. Ray Gerber, St. Joseph's College, Windham, Maine

Library of Congress Cataloging-in-Publication Data
Cerullo, Mary M.
Coral reef : a city that never sleeps / text by Mary M. Cerullo ;
photographs by Jeffrey L. Rotman.
p.   cm.
Includes bibliographical references (p.   ) and index.
ISBN 0–525–65193–4
1. Coral reef biology—Juvenile literature.   2. Coral reef ecology—
Juvenile literature.   3. Corals—Juvenile literature. 4. Coral reefs and islands—
Juvenile literature.   [1. Coral reef ecology.   2. Ecology.   3. Coral reefs and islands.]
I. Rotman, Jeffrey L., ill.   II. Title.
QH95.8.C47   1996   574.9′1—dc20   95–6635   CIP   AC

Published in the United States by Cobblehill Books,
an affiliate of Dutton Children's Books,
a division of Penguin Books USA Inc.,
375 Hudson Street, New York, New York 10014

Designed by Charlotte Staub
Printed in Hong Kong
First Edition   10 9 8 7 6 5 4 3 2 1

Contents

Brightly colored Anthias *fish swarm over soft coral.*

CHAPTER 1

Living Treasures
of the Sea

Tropical seas once sheltered pirate strongholds heaped high with treasures plundered from unlucky merchant ships. Today, anyone with a snorkel or a scuba tank can find underwater treasures as dazzling, and as dangerous, as any pirate's den. Jewel-like fishes dart past ruby-colored sponges, emerald corals, and sapphire sea fans. Snails, crabs, and shrimp creep through limestone tunnels. Finned assassins, armed with razor-sharp teeth, lurk among the shadows. This is the coral reef,

The rainbow wrasse displays bold colors.

where weirdly shaped "plants" and "shrubs" are actually the skeletons of millions of sea animals.

Corals grow in colonies or clumps, their shape determined by the kind of coral and by how deep they live. Their names create a vivid image of the variety of shapes on the reef: finger coral, brain coral, cabbage coral, cactus coral. Corals that grow close to the surface, such as elkhorn coral and staghorn coral, may have many branches to capture sunlight from every angle. Plate corals often live in deeper water, and they fan out like satellite dishes to capture the stray rays of sunshine that penetrate the depths.

Soft corals, swaying in the ocean current, animate the reef. The broad sea fans or scraggly sea whips and wire corals have flexible internal skeletons that allow them to bend without breaking.

The many inhabitants of the coral reef find food and shelter among the coral branches, boulders, fingers, and fans. Tube worms and sea anemones cling to the tall spires and rounded domes, while gaudy angelfishes, triggerfishes, and damselfishes flutter like bright banners above the coral formations. Sea urchins, sea stars, octopuses, eels, and schools of bigeye fishes pass the daylight hours in coral caves or crevices, or under rocky ledges along the reef wall. At night, while the colorful reef fishes rest inside their coral chambers, these other residents roam a coral city that never sleeps.

Staghorn corals often have delicate colors.

Plate corals grow in deep water, but spread out like a fan to capture any rays of sunlight.

Coral reefs are restricted to a belt 3,000 miles wide that encircles the equator. Reef-building corals thrive on the eastern shores of large land masses like Australia and Indonesia, around small islands like those in the Caribbean Sea, and in tropical waters like the Red Sea and the Indian Ocean. Coral reefs cover 80 million square miles, or 25 times the area of the United States. The longest coral reef is the Great Barrier Reef off the east coast of Australia. It stretches for 1,250 miles.

A reef that grows on rocks along the shore is called a *fringing reef.* A *barrier reef* grows farther offshore, separated from land by a shallow, sandy lagoon. An *atoll* is an irregularly shaped ring of coral with a lagoon

The branches of soft corals are tough but flexible, and bend in strong currents, like trees in the wind.

in the middle. Atolls are primarily found in deep water in the Indian and Pacific oceans. Small, isolated reefs, called *patch reefs*, are found in some shallow, tropical waters.

A coral polyp feeds at night, stretching its tentacles out to capture any food that comes its way.

CHAPTER 2

Builders of the Reef

$\mathcal{T}$he chief architect of the coral reef is a creature no larger than a pea. It is the coral *polyp* (POL-up), a soft, fleshy animal that resembles an upside-down jellyfish. A slitlike mouth takes in food and gets rid of wastes. Surrounding it are stinging tentacles with poison-tipped harpoons that the polyp shoots out to capture prey that comes within its range. The coral feeds on *zooplankton*—newly hatched shrimp, crabs, fish, and sea worms and other microscopic creatures that float in the currents of the sea.

The coral polyp lives inside a circular stone house called a *corallite*. The outer skin of the polyp has special cells that are able to take calcium carbonate from seawater and deposit it as a hard cup around the body of the polyp. This solid limestone cup cements the polyp to the reef. (Calcium carbonate also forms the shells of snails, clams, and crabs.) By day, the coral polyp curls up inside its limestone shelter. By night, it stretches up out of the corallite and spreads its tentacles to capture the zooplankton food that comes its way.

It is the coral polyp skeleton that builds the reef. Long after the coral polyp dies, the corallite remains attached to the reef. Billions of these coral skeletons, many as ancient as the Pyramids, make up some of the oldest, largest, and most beautiful structures on Earth.

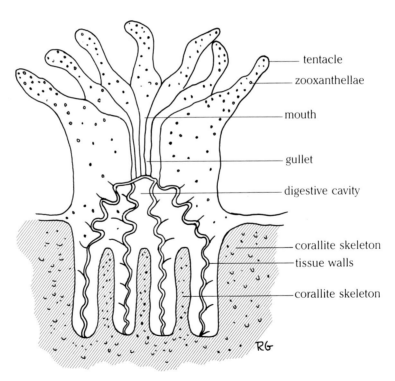

Diagram of a coral polyp

Even though these coral polyps hide during the daytime and open up to feed in the darkness of night, sunlight is important to them. That is because they house many microscopic plant guests called *zooxanthellae* (zoh-uh-zan-THEL-ee). Coral polyps could not build a coral reef without the help of these plant companions. Zooxanthellae speed up the process by which coral polyps can remove calcium carbonate from the seawater.

Like all plants, zooxanthellae use the energy from the sun to change water and carbon dioxide into oxygen, sugars, and starches. This is the process of *photosynthesis*. The zooxanthellae use the wastes from the polyp—carbon dioxide and nitrates—to help them grow. In return, the plants supply food and oxygen to the polyp. In some cases, the zooxanthellae may provide almost all of a coral polyp's food supply. The rest of the polyp's diet consists of the tiny animals it harpoons with dartlike threads, called *nematocysts*, fired from its stinging tentacles.

Corals grow by budding, as plants do. A coral polyp can branch off an exact duplicate of itself. These polyps do not break loose, but remain attached to the parent polyp and build limestone corallites of their own. Gradually, they add to the coral, branching upward and outward bit by bit, slowly enlarging the reef.

Coral polyps can also produce eggs which, after they are fertilized, float through the water until they settle on rocks or dead coral to create new coral reefs. Great numbers of eggs are produced at one time, but few survive because many sea creatures find them a tasty meal.

A coral reef will only flourish where there is
- clear, fairly shallow water, so that the zooxanthellae can get sunlight
- waves or currents to deliver food and oxygen to the coral polyp
- warm temperatures, ideally 75°–85° F. (24°–30° C.)
- salty sea water

The sea anemone is closely related to corals and jellyfish. They all use stinging tentacles to snare small, floating sea creatures.

Stony corals like brain coral and staghorn coral and the soft corals like sea whips and sea fans belong to the same group or phylum: *Cnidaria* (nie-DAR-ee-a). This phylum also includes sea anemones, jellyfish, and hydra. Because soft corals don't depend on small plants living within them, they can survive in total darkness in caves or on the deep seafloor where stony corals can't. But only the stony corals can build a reef.

A reef is not just made of coral skeletons. Pink coralline algae, a seaweed that also takes calcium carbonate from seawater, cements sea urchin spines, seashells, worm casings, and other remains of sea animals onto the reef. Seaweeds and sponges also add to the reef.

What the reef builders create, others tear down. Parrotfishes, damselfishes, some crabs, snails, mussels, worms, sea urchins, and boring sponges scrape, tunnel, and hollow out the reef. They help create coral sand, which collects between colonies of corals, in shallow lagoons, and on the beaches of coral islands. The sand provides homes or feeding grounds for many reef animals.

No one will challenge this hermit crab for its place on the reef. Most others avoid the sting of the fire coral it is perched on.

CHAPTER 3

Cities in the Sea

*I*n many ways, a coral reef is like a city: busy, crowded, and colorful. The reef supplies food, protection, and social life for the creatures that squeeze into every available living space. Reef residents live at many different levels, like apartment dwellers in high-rise buildings. Once an animal sets up housekeeping in one area, it rarely moves unless it is evicted by a new tenant. New housing is hard to find. Many coral reefs are more densely populated than the largest cities on Earth.

This crab seems reluctant to leave its hiding place on the coral reef, where good homes are hard to find.

Why are coral reefs so crowded? We think of tropical seas as rich, lush environments, but compared to cold, northern waters, there is very little life floating in them. Tropical waters are crystal clear because they contain so few plankton, minerals, decaying plants, and other nutrients that plants and animals need to survive. A coral reef is like a city in a tropical desert—an oasis—which may provide the only food and shelter for miles around. The fishes, crabs, and other inhabitants contend for a limited food supply: microscopic plants and animals carried in by the waves, green mats of seaweed on dead coral, or other reef residents.

Each coral colony can support only a small number of animals that require the same kinds of food and shelter. Competition is fierce on the coral reef. A single pair of butterflyfish, which may feed only on the

The bright colors of these butterflyfish are thought to make it easier for them to defend their territory.

The enormous eyes of the bigeye scad pick out any movement on the night reef. Its red coloration appears black in dark water.

tentacles of feather-duster worms, may live above a particular coral boulder. The fishes' bold stripes and aggressive behavior warn others of the same species that they are not welcome on this patch of reef. Specializations in habits, diet, and color allow each animal to carve out its own very special niche, or position, in the community.

One way reef dwellers have been able to share the limited resources of the reef is by maintaining different schedules. If you were to visit a coral reef by day and then return to the same reef after dark, you would meet two entirely different sets of inhabitants. As one animal wiggles out of its den in the reef to search for food, another crawls into the same retreat to rest.

There are three distinct periods of activity on the reef—the day shift, the night shift, and an in-between time at dawn and dusk when the shifts are changing. Scientists estimate that one-half to two-thirds of all species of reef fishes are *diurnal*, that is, active by day. These include brightly colored fishes such as butterflyfishes, angelfishes, triggerfishes, and clownfishes. Many have well-developed eyes which can detect color. They communicate by color to attract a mate, to advertise a service, or to claim their own part of the reef.

About 10 percent of all reef fish species are *crepuscular*, which means they are most active at dawn and dusk. These are primarily the large predators that roam the reef. They will take victims any time of the day, but prey are easier to catch as the shifts change. Some fish are not as alert to danger as they should be as they wearily return home after many hours of foraging for food, or as they set off to begin a new day. Reef sharks, barracuda, groupers, and jacks pick off any stragglers that fall behind the rush-hour crowd.

Another one-quarter to one-third of coral reef fishes rest by day and hunt by night. These *nocturnal* animals prowl a world without light, and rely on their keen senses of smell, taste, and touch. Some have huge eyes to help pierce the darkness. Owl-eyed squirrelfishes, cardinalfishes, and bigeye scads emerge at night from underneath the coral ledges where they huddle by day.

Many of the reef's *invertebrates*—animals without backbones—also come out at night. Coral polyps poke their tentacles above their stony cups, safe for a time from the prying lips of daytime fishes. Crabs, spiny lobsters, and sea urchins fan out across the ocean floor to scavenge for food. An octopus glides back to its den with a crab. Populated by shadowy figures, the nocturnal reef is a lively mix of predators and prey.

A butterflyfish has to respect its neighbor's territory.

CHAPTER 4

The Day Shift

At first glance, the daytime reef seems on the verge of chaos. Dozens of fishes mill about a coral boulder. The growing crowd attracts still others. In the midst of this confusion, a delicate shrimp can be seen heading straight into the gaping jaws of a moray eel.

A few feet away, a brawl breaks out when a butterflyfish crosses an invisible line dividing its turf from its neighbor's. The commotion scares a small tomato clownfish into the waiting tentacles of a deadly sea anemone. Above the reef, schools of fishes rush back and forth without any apparent purpose.

Gradually, though, if you watch and wait, order appears out of the chaos. The butterflyfish is merely defending its home as the clownfish retreats to his. The coral boulder is a cleaning station where fishes wait their turn for service. The cleaner shrimp picks parasites off the teeth of a customer, the moray eel. The schools of fishes travel familiar routes between feeding and resting areas, ever alert to dangers along the way.

Color Sends a Signal

Make a spectacle of yourself, and chances are you will be noticed. That doesn't seem to make good survival sense in the sea, because as soon as an animal gets noticed, it usually gets eaten. Yet there are hundreds of gaudy exhibitionists parading around the coral reef. Bold stripes of black and white compete for attention with neon spots and splashes of blue, yellow, green, and red.

Why do these colorful creatures seem to purposely put themselves in danger? Scientists believe that the animals' distinctive markings show their place in the community. Their vivid colors communicate messages of welcome, courtship, or warning. Some reef fishes can even change their color when they are excited, angry, or threatened.

Some sport dazzling colors to attract a mate. Since there may be only a few royal angelfishes on any particular reef, it's important for a male royal angelfish and a female royal angelfish to be able to find each other among the crowd. (Otherwise there wouldn't be any future little royal angelfishes.)

Distinctive coloring may warn others that certain animals are dan-

The angelfish relies on dramatic colors to attract a mate.

gerous or that they taste bad. A lionfish has poison sacs embedded in the fins on its back and sides. When confronted by an enemy, it erects its boldly striped fins, possibly to warn the potential predator that this meal is not worth dying for.

But not everyone on the reef wants to be noticed. The scorpionfish is even more venomous than its flamboyant cousin, the lionfish. Instead of darting around the reef, it sits quietly on the ocean floor among seaweeds or coral rubble. Since it is camouflaged to look like part of the coral reef, most crabs, fishes, and other victims never know what swallowed them. Other fishes use stripes and splotches of colors—

The venomous back spines of the scorpionfish can be deadly to a diver or to a fish that blunders into it on the ocean floor.

disruptive coloration—to break up the body's silhouette and help them blend in with the vibrant, multihued coral reef.

There are so many hiding places in the reef that being gaudy is not usually a problem. An escape route is always nearby. The shape of a typical coral reef fish—flat and round like a compact disc—allows it to slip effortlessly into any coral crevice. A fairly large tail and short side fins help the fish to brake, swerve, or reverse direction in the blink of an eye.

Good eyesight and color vision are important advantages for daytime fishes. Sharp hearing, keen sense of smell, and unusual alliances also help them meet the challenges of diurnal living on the coral reef.

Cleaners and Other Partners

Some animals use color to advertise their services. Many species of gobies, wrasses, and other cleaner fishes sport black or electric blue stripes that run the length of their bodies. Like a barber's pole, the stripes are the signs of their profession. A cleaner fish removes annoying parasites that irritate the skin, mouth, and gills of larger fishes. In return, the cleaner fish gets to eat the parasites.

As a prospective customer approaches a cleaning station, a cleaner fish usually rushes up with an effusive greeting. The cleaner fish zigzags back and forth in front of the larger fish—perhaps combining an urge to flee and the desire to feed. A candy cane cleaner shrimp waves its long antennae back and forth in the water to attract business. A client may signal that it wants attention by changing color, standing on its head or

This cleaner fish goes right inside the mouth of the moray eel to pick parasites from its teeth.

23

tail, or by "yawning." Other, less demonstrative fish simply wait in line.

A cleaner may move right inside a fish's mouth to clean between its teeth. Good intentions aren't always rewarded, however, as sometimes the cleaner gets consumed.

On the whole, the cleaning strategy works so well that imitators sometimes set up shop near cleaning stations. False cleaners, called "mimics," have adopted color patterns and movements similar to those of real cleaners in order to get close to larger fish. Then, instead of nibbling parasites, the mimics take a bite out of the customer's fins. Generally, only young fish get fooled this way.

Cleaning "clinics" may help keep the reef healthy by removing dead skin, parasites, or fungus from sick or wounded fishes. Many fishes of the reef take advantage of this service. Some return several times a day to have their injuries treated. One cleaner wrasse treated 300 fishes in six hours! A human doctor who tried to serve that many patients in one day would probably collapse from exhaustion.

Color and visual recognition are critical to their advertising, so cleaner fishes and cleaner shrimp close up shop for the night to make sure that no one mistakes their overtures for cleaning as invitations to dine.

The partnership formed by the cleaner and its customer is an example of *symbiosis*. Symbiosis means, literally, "living together." It is the relationship between two different species in which at least one benefits. A guide dog leading a blind human would be an example of symbiosis you might find on land. These partnerships abound on the coral reef.

Some of them are very strange. Even given the housing shortage on the coral reef, what animal would choose to live among the deadly tentacles of a sea anemone? The clownfish depends on it, and appears to avoid being stung by its venomous host by taking the time to get acquainted. It gently nuzzles against the anemone. Scientists are still

This clownfish has found a safe refuge within a sea anemone, whose stinging tentacles ward off any pursuers.

trying to figure out whether the fish coats itself with the anemone's slimy mucus (which prevents the anemone from stinging itself), or if it triggers a chemical change in the fish's own mucus covering that makes it immune to the sting. The clownfish, and eventually its mate, rarely stray more than a few feet from their host. They chase all other clownfishes away, although they may lure other kinds of fishes into the anemone's deadly grasp.

Territories

The angelfish could give lessons on how to beat the competition for food, space, and mates on a coral reef. Some species of angelfishes have developed a taste for only certain kinds of sponges or seaweeds. An individual angelfish hovers close to its food source and hiding place and defends them from all others interested in similar food, shelter, or nesting sites. Its bright warning colors are posted like a No Trespassing sign. Many angelfish have solved the mating problem by pairing with one other angelfish for life. Together, they vigorously defend their territory.

In many species of coral fishes, color patterns change from youth to adulthood. Juvenile angelfish often wear totally different colors than the adults of the same species. Perhaps this disguises them from predators or lets them move freely across adult angelfishes' territories. Perhaps the juveniles don't yet present a direct threat for space, food, or mates. As young angelfish mature into their grown-up colors, their trespassing is no longer tolerated by other angelfish.

Feeding Adaptations

As diets become more specialized, many coral reef fishes have evolved "tools" for feeding. The long-nosed butterflyfish pries into crevices in the reef to grab worms, tiny shrimp, and coral polyps with a mouth shaped like a pair of long-nosed pliers.

A triggerfish exposes the vulnerable underside of a sea urchin by shooting a stream of water, like a fire hose, across the urchin's long spines. The strong teeth and jaws of the triggerfish can chisel through the hard shells of mussels, oysters, clams, and crabs.

Anchoring itself to a coral branch with its tail, the sea horse sucks shrimp and plankton out of the water with jaws shaped like a hollow straw. Because the sea horse has no stomach to store food, it has to eat constantly. A young sea horse may slurp up as many as 3,500 shrimp in a day.

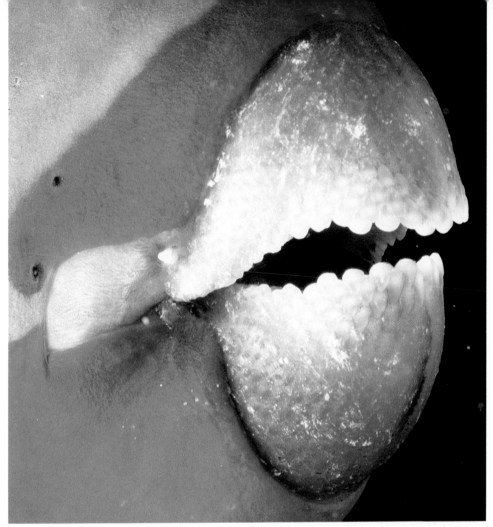

The parrotfish is one of the noisiest creatures on the daytime reef. It loudly crunches coral with teeth that have fused together.

The parrotfish has a mouth made for munching. It is a most useful tool because it recycles the reef. This fish's teeth have fused together into a strong scraper that knocks off chunks of coral. The parrotfish feeds on the algae that grows on dead coral or on the zooxanthellae in living coral. These coral scrapings are ground up by a second set of teeth in the parrotfish's throat and passed out the other end, creating coral sand for tropical beaches. A study in Bermuda concluded that for every acre of coral reef, one *ton* of coral skeletons was converted into sand each year, primarily through the feeding habits of parrotfishes.

A school of Anthias *returns late in the day. Each will head to its individual hiding place in the coral.*

CHAPTER 5

The Twilight Reef

*B*y late afternoon, the daytime fishes become less interested in feeding and start to move closer to their evening retreats. Perhaps they grow nervous as their day vision becomes less efficient at dusk. The smallest fishes start the rush hour to return to their shelters for the night. Soon others follow their example.

The bright colors of the diurnal fishes fade fast in the twilight. Some fishes can actually adjust color cells in their skin to alter their flashy

A parrotfish settles down for the night inside a mucus "sleeping bag" that seals its scent from predators.

daytime look to dull, darker night shades. The gathering gloom just makes others appear darker. The best defense is to disappear entirely inside the coral reef, because now the fishes' dark outlines are silhouetted against the setting sun to predators below.

Parrotfishes leave their feeding grounds in single file to seek out their individual hiding places in the reef. Some parrotfishes secrete a sticky cocoon from beneath their scales to seal their scent from hungry moray eels. If any creature tries to penetrate the mucus bubble, the parrotfish wakes up and bolts from its "bedroom." Some species of wrasses also make cocoons for the night. Others bury themselves in the sand.

Because fishes don't have eyelids to close, it's impossible to tell whether or not most fishes are really sleeping. Parrotfishes do seem to go into a trancelike state at night. If they are disturbed from their rest, they act dazed and confused, like humans wakened out of a sound sleep.

A triggerfish locks itself inside a coral cave with a tall spine on its back fin. One spine folds down over the first spine like a door latch to hold it in place. Only the triggerfish can release its trigger spine, so a moray eel can't pull it from its retreat.

Shadow Patrols

Many carnivores, such as jacks, snappers, sharks, barracuda, and groupers, take advantage of the weariness and confusion of transition time on the reef. Their eyes, sensitive to dim light, are better equipped for this time of day than those of the diurnal fishes. Though twilight predators are not very good at distinguishing colors, they can detect shape, outlines, and movement well. The daytime fishes flowing back to the reef offer a constant stream of shape and movement.

Many predators that have been quietly waiting in the background all day become more active at dusk and dawn. The crepuscular hunters have ingenious ways of picking off their prey. A grouper leaves its den beneath a coral overhang to vacuum up prey with its cavernous mouth. By thrusting out its lower jaw, its mouth becomes big enough to swallow almost any prey. It has been rumored that giant groupers (which may weigh up to 1,000 pounds) have been known to swallow divers whole! Then, the stories go, they spit them out again because they don't like the taste of their wetsuits.

Streamlined jacks hunt in packs like jackals. They surround a school of fish, separate several from their companions, and bring them down

A school of jacks prepares to ambush weary fish traveling between their feeding grounds and their sleeping shelters.

A lionfish spreads its side fins to herd smaller fishes against a reef wall.

after a high-speed chase. A lionfish may use its winglike side fins to sweep fish into a corner of the reef where they can't escape. Other times, it lies motionless and gulps fish that come too close.

Although sharks visit the coral reef at dawn and dusk, they have such an effective array of sensory devices that they can zero in on prey at any time. Their excellent sense of smell has earned sharks the nickname of "swimming noses." Sharks' lateral lines are especially sensitive to the low-frequency vibrations given off by struggling fishes. Their most impressive sense is located inside sensory pores on the snout. This sense detects the faint electric pulses generated by the beating hearts of their victims. Vision is probably their weakest sense, yet many sharks have catlike eyes with mirror cells to reflect and concentrate dim light. Some sharks' eyes are so sensitive that they can hunt by starlight on a moonless evening.

Dusk, that time between twilight and full darkness, is the spawning time for many diurnal fishes. As one scientist explains, "It gives their eggs and sperm a twelve-hour head start to escape the hungry mouths on the reef." Many daytime fishes move into deeper water, rise to the surface, or spawn during outgoing tides to let ocean currents carry their eggs and sperm to less populated areas far from the reef.

Ghost Town

About ten minutes after sunset, an eerie quiet descends on the reef. Swaying sea fans provide the only visible movement, like tumbleweeds blowing through a ghost town in a Western movie. The coral passages are silent, deserted, and vaguely menacing. The daytime fishes have retreated to their shelters. Many large predators have headed off with the setting sun into the deeper waters beyond the reef. Others—some groupers, snappers, and reef sharks—remain hidden in the shadows where they can ambush any lone stragglers.

The quiet period lasts only about 15 to 20 minutes. Then, as abruptly as if a film director had shouted "Cut!" nocturnal creatures burst onto the set and the scene changes to night maneuvers.

A crinoid, or feather star, perches atop a fire coral at night to trap plankton with its sticky tube feet.

CHAPTER 6

Night of the Living Reef

The sun clings briefly to the horizon, a glowing ball burning a fire trail across the water. Then, almost as soon as the sun disappears, the sky turns black and starry.

Now the coral reef literally unfolds. Coral polyps pump themselves full of seawater to stretch their tentacles beyond the ridges of their stony cups. Their stinging tentacles are poised to harpoon any passing plankton. Delicate tube worms unfurl their tentacles to take in food and

A brittle star is so delicate that its arms break off at the slightest touch.

oxygen. Wherever you turn on the reef, invertebrates—animals without backbones—are emerging from hiding.

Crinoids, basket stars, and brittle stars spread their feathery arms and position themselves where they can feast on plankton. Spiny sea urchins shake themselves loose from the reef and head off toward the reef lagoon for a night of grazing. Sea urchins and sea stars have primitive sight organs that are able to distinguish light from dark. Wave your hand over a spiny sea urchin, and its spines will follow the shadow of your palm.

Many brittle stars light up at night like twinkling stars. They may flash up to 50 times a minute. No one knows for sure why certain creatures produce their own light. Maybe the flashing lights attract prey, startle predators, or warn others that this animal tastes bad.

Nudibranchs, like this striped pajama nudibranch, may look defenseless, but they have an arsenal of chemical weapons.

Nudibranchs—"sea slugs"—pirouette through the water. These shell-less mollusks seem defenseless, but they have evolved creative ways to repel attackers. Some nudibranchs swallow the stinging cells of sea anemones whole. They store them, undigested and unfired, in the gills on their backs. Later, they can use them for their own protection. Other nudibranchs ooze toxic chemicals—sulphuric acid or poisonous slime—from their skin.

Fishes that feed on invertebrates soon appear. Grunts, drumfishes, and squirrelfishes all make a noisy racket as they head off to feed in the sandy lagoon or in the deep water beyond the reef. Grunts stir up worms, shrimps, and other sand dwellers. Squirrelfishes hunt along the steep reef wall for zooplankton—tiny, drifting animals such as fish eggs or just-hatched crabs, sea stars, or jellyfish.

The bug-eyes of squirrelfishes, soldierfishes, and bigeye scads seek out motion rather than images. Millions of years ago, when dinosaurs ruled the Earth, these fishes lived on the coral reef and were probably active during the day. As the dinosaurs died out on land, new species of fishes were emerging in the sea. Many of the newcomers evolved feeding mechanisms and excellent eyesight that made them better able to compete for space on the daytime reef. Scientists think that the "modern" fishes eventually crowded out the more primitive squirrelfishes until they were confined to the night shift.

The moray eel and the octopus are true creatures of the night. Both use highly developed senses other than eyesight. The octopus relies on touch and taste. Each of an octopus' eight arms is lined with sensitive suction cups that not only grab prey but can taste it as well. The rims of these suction cups are loaded with sensory organs that can detect sweet, sour, and bitter tastes better than the human tongue. They can even distinguish a live clam from a dead one.

The glassy eyes of a bigeye scad penetrate the gloom as it heads out to hunt for plankton beyond the reef.

To escape a moray eel's attack, an octopus can change color, squirt a cloud of ink, and jet-propel itself backwards. It may even break off an arm as a last resort.

The octopus is the moray's favorite meal. Squeezing its sinuous body through narrow tunnels in the reef, it tracks an octopus to its hidden den. An acute sense of smell leads the moray eel to its prey. Taste buds around the eel's mouth trigger it to attack. Viselike jaws and backward-pointing teeth lock onto an arm of the octopus, but the octopus has a trick to play. It breaks off its arm to escape. (The octopus will grow a new one.) Then the octopus squirts a cloud of ink and mucus, shaped like the octopus, that hangs in the water for several seconds. The real thing, meanwhile, changes color and jet-propels in the opposite direction. Some scientists think the ink screen may briefly numb the moray's sense of smell.

Sometimes neighboring colonies of corals battle for living space. A large fungus coral, for example, might live peacefully next to a cactus coral by day. But at night, the fungus coral sends out poison darts to stab, sting, and digest its neighbor. White scars of exposed coral skeletons show where the cactus coral was wounded. The attacker sometimes completely overgrows the weaker coral colony. Scientists who have witnessed these coral wars report that only colonies of different species attack each other, never two colonies of the same species.

Breeding

The nighttime activities of corals also have a gentler side. Triggered by rising water temperatures, phases of the moon, or the tides, corals release their eggs and sperm at night. Some corals have eggs, some have sperm, some have both. Because plankton-eating fish would gobble up these clouds of eggs and sperm during the day, night is the safest time to stage this event.

Sexual reproduction is the way corals launch new colonies. A fertilized egg soon hatches into larva called a *planula*. The planula drifts for several days and finally plops down onto a hard, clean surface. It immediately begins to build a skeleton to anchor itself to the rock. The planula changes from a shapeless blob into a polyp with a stalk and tentacles. From then on, the polyp is attached for life. It will grow by budding, cloning new polyps just like itself.

More new life will be created this night. A mother sea turtle crosses the reef to reach a nearby coral beach. Although she spends the rest of

A mother sea turtle heads to shore to lay her eggs under cover of darkness.

her life at sea, she must lay her eggs on land. She may migrate thousands of miles to return to the beach of her birth, which she recognizes by smell or by some other clue scientists don't yet fully understand.

The female sea turtle is a graceful swimmer in the ocean, but her huge bulk makes her slow and clumsy on land. Her heavy shell pushes against her lungs, making it difficult for her to breathe. She gulps air in short, labored puffs as she drags herself up the beach to the high tide line.

She digs a hole in the moist sand to cradle a hundred slippery, Ping-Pong ball-sized eggs. The mother turtle carefully covers the hole and packs the sand down with her shell. Finally, she shovels dirt loosely all around with her front flippers to hide the nest from predators and poachers. She lumbers back down the beach, her job done. The babies are on their own. Once they hatch, they'll face a gauntlet of seabirds, crabs, and lizards as they scramble across the sand to the sea.

The first shafts of sunlight fall across the reef as the mother turtle slips beneath the waves. Coral polyps shrink inside their stony shelters. Soldierfishes, cardinalfishes, and other creatures of the night retreat to the shadows beneath coral ledges. Another day has begun.

Pollution, overfishing, and the building of seaside homes and hotels threaten fragile coral reefs, like this atoll in Palau, Micronesia.

CHAPTER 7

A Cloudy Future

*A*round the world, many coral reefs that once pulsed with color and activity now are nearly deserted. A fuzzy blanket of green algae covers bleached, dead coral. Coral reefs could someday disappear. Today, they are dynamited for food fish, poisoned to capture aquarium specimens, blasted for construction, polluted by sewage, and smothered by silt.

Many reefs have turned ghostly white from *coral bleaching*, a natural disaster in which most or all of the corals' plant partners, the zooxanthellae, are ejected from their hosts. In conditions of above- or below-normal water temperatures, runoff of fresh water, silt, or too little sunlight, the coral polyps may react by getting rid of their plant partners (or the plants may leave on their own and swim by means of a threadlike tail to find a new host). Without the plants, the transparent polyps lose all their color and, more importantly, their ability to build more reef.

Scientists are trying to understand why coral bleaching happens. Pollution and global warming have been blamed. Many recent cases of coral bleaching appear to be tied to an increase in water temperatures.

This candy cane sea star, and other animals that depend on healthy coral reefs, may disappear if their homes do.

Huge schools of fish, like these glassy sweepers, are killed by dynamiting or poisoning the reefs.

Some people suspect these are the early signs of global warming, a condition in which too much heat may be trapped in the Earth's atmosphere from the burning of coal, oil, and natural gas. This would be too bad for the coral reefs, but also for the rest of the planet. Healthy coral reefs may actually slow global warming by removing carbon dioxide from the atmosphere.

In a survey done in the 1980s, 97 of 103 countries with coral reefs

49

Large specimens of the giant Tridacna *clam, like this one in the Red Sea, are becoming rare. Coral reef sanctuaries will help protect them.*

reported that their coral communities had already suffered damage. In the Pacific and Indian oceans, fishermen dynamite the reefs. Stunned fishes float to the surface where they are easily scooped into fishing boats. Fishermen, particularly in the Philippines, use poison to collect exotic coral reef fish for aquarium hobbyists. They squirt sodium cyanide into holes in the reef to drive the fishes from their hiding places. Some fishes die immediately. Up to 80 percent of the rest will die from the effects of the poison within a few weeks or months.

Damage can be done by well-meaning visitors. A diver may accidentally kick the coral with his flipper, breaking off a delicate coral branch that will take years to grow back. Boats damage the reef when they drag or drop their anchors over coral. On tropical islands, the construction of seaside homes, resorts, and dive camps excavates sand and silt that then flow out onto the reef. These sediments cloud the water and smother the coral. Sewage from shoreline homes and hotels can also pollute the reef. The natural fertilizers in sewage trigger the rapid growth of algae that soon die off and rob the water of oxygen and light.

What can be done to help coral reefs? Environmental organizations are campaigning for better protection of the reefs. Citizens and legislators push for laws creating coral reef sanctuaries. Divers, boaters, and sightseers visiting coral reefs are beginning to police themselves. Many pet store owners now demand that their suppliers guarantee that tropical fishes are collected humanely.

Even people far from coral reefs can come to their aid. We can help make the atmosphere and oceans cleaner by using less energy and by keeping pollutants out of water. The "Three R's"—reduce, reuse, and recycle—help not just our own communities, but the coral reef communities on the other side of the globe. Even if we never visit one of these cities under the sea, we can still be good neighbors.

Glossary

algae Seaweeds or one-celled plants.

atoll An irregularly shaped ring of coral reef enclosing a lagoon.

barrier reef A coral reef separated from shore by a lagoon.

budding An asexual form of reproduction that adds new members of the coral colony, similar to cloning.

calcium carbonate A compound found in limestone, marble, coral skeletons, crab shells, teeth, bones, and dissolved in seawater.

Cnidaria The phylum, or group, which includes corals, sea anemones, jellyfish, and hydras. The name refers to the stinging cells they all have in common. (This phylum is also sometimes called Coelenterata, meaning "hollow-gut.")

coral bleaching A natural disaster in which most or all of the corals' plant partners, the zooxanthellae, are ejected from their hosts.

corallite The limestone cup that a coral polyp makes by taking calcium carbonate from seawater.

crepuscular Most active at dawn and dusk, such as reef sharks and mosquitoes.

disruptive coloration A kind of camouflage where varying colors and patterns break up the body's outline.

diurnal Active during the day, like butterflyfishes and butterflies; comes from the Latin word for "day."

fringing reef A coral reef that runs along the shoreline.

global warming The theory that carbon dioxide and other gases produced by burning fossil fuels are trapped in the upper atmosphere, absorbing and reflecting heat back to earth.

invertebrate Animal without a backbone. Ninety-five percent of all animals in the sea are invertebrates.

nematocyst   A coiled thread inside a stinging cell that is fired on contact and harpoons prey.

niche   The particular role of an individual species in a community, including its place in the food chain, its living space, and its behavior.

nocturnal   Active during the night, like stony coral polyps.

nudibranch   A shell-less snail with external gills; a sea slug.

patch reef   A coral boulder or clump of corals unattached to a larger reef system.

photosynthesis   How plants use the energy of the sunlight to convert water and carbon dioxide into sugars, starches, and oxygen.

plankton   Literally "wanderer." One-celled drifting plants and tiny floating animals which include microscopic animals as well as the larval stage of many sea creatures, such as crabs, sea stars, and fish.

planula   The young, free-swimming stage of a coral.

polyp   The nonswimming stage of a coral or sea anemone. The animal looks like a hollow cup with tentacles surrounding its open end.

symbiosis   Means literally "living together." Two different species live together in a relationship in which at least one benefits; for example, coral polyps and zooxanthellae.

territory   A specific area that an animal defends from intruders, especially those competing for the same food, mates, shelter, or space.

zooplankton   Animal plankton.

zooxanthellae   One-celled algae living in the tissues of reef-building corals, as well as in some sea anemones, *Tridacna* clams, and sponges.

Bibliography

Juvenile Titles

Arnold, Caroline. *A Walk on the Great Barrier Reef*. Carolrhoda, Minneapolis, MN, 1988

Barrett, Norman. *Coral Reef*. Franklin Watts, New York, 1991

Bender, Lionel. *Life on a Coral Reef*. Franklin Watts, New York, 1989

George, Michael. *Coral Reef*. Creative Education, Inc., Mankato, MN, 1992

Gilbreath, Alice Thompson, *The Great Barrier Reef: A Treasure in the Sea*. Dillon Press, Minneapolis, MN, 1986

Jacobson, Morris K. and David R. Franz. *Wonders of Corals and Coral Reefs*. Dodd, Mead, New York, 1979

Johnson, Sylvia A. *Coral Reefs*. Lerner Publications, Minneapolis, MN, 1984

Sargent, William. *Night Reef: Dusk to Dawn on a Coral Reef*. Franklin Watts, New York, 1991

Tayntor, Elizabeth, Paul Erickson, and Les Kaufman. *Dive to the Coral Reefs*. Crown Publishers, New York, 1986

Look Closer: Coral Reef. Dorling Kindersley, Inc., New York, 1992

Adult Titles

Halliday, Les. *Coral Reefs*. Tetra Press, Morris Plains, NJ, 1989

Kaplan, Eugene H. *A Field Guide to Coral Reefs of the Caribbean and Florida*. Houghton Mifflin, Boston, 1982

Levine, Joseph S. *The Coral Reef at Night*. Harry N. Abrams, Inc., New York, 1993

Sale, Peter F., ed. *The Ecology of Fishes on Coral Reefs*. Academic Press, San Diego, CA, 1991

Wells, Sue and Nick Hanna. *The Greenpeace Book of Coral Reefs*. Sterling Publishing Co., New York, 1992

Wilson, Roberta and James Q. Wilson. *Watching Fishes: Life and Behavior on Coral Reefs*. Harper & Row, New York, 1985

Index